Star in the custard

NICOLA DAVIES
illustrated by Elaine Franks

Children need poetry from day one. It isn't a luxury.
It's a necessity like healthy food and exercise. It's top
quality brain food. It's essential shared experience with
adults and other children. And it's fun.

Especially enjoyable are spiky, imaginative poems for
children like the ones Nicola Davies has written for this
book and which Elaine Franks has brought cheerfully to
life with her big-eyed, brightly-coloured illustrations.

The real thrill of poetry is its limitless scope. You can go
anywhere in a poem. 'Seeking Silver' and 'The Witches go
Shopping' are real adventures. Even going to bed becomes
a journey of exploration in 'The Sleepmaster'. Suddenly
the mundane is magical.

Yes, readers of this book really will find that there's a star
awaiting them in the custard.

Susan Elkin

Introduction

We're Bethan and Gareth and Gwilym the Kid
   And these are poems of things that we did.
We twins are Year Four and Gwilym is two
   And these are our poems of things that we do.

There are poems to scare you and ones that are fun
   And things we imagine and things we have done
With Dylan our dog and our kitten, Big Sid,
   Even poems of Grandpa and Gwilym the Kid.

Some poems rhyme and some of them don't,
   Some will amuse you . . . and some of them won't!
   The rhythms are catchy, the verses are new
     – All of them written from us to you.

Contents

The Topsy-Turvy Man

If you go walking up the lane
You'll meet the most curious fella.
Although there's not a cloud in sight
It's raining inside his umbrella.

He wears his jacket upside down
His gloves are on his toes
He always knows just where he's been
But never where he goes.

And when rain pours with all its might
He folds up his umbrella
For where he is the sun shines bright
On that topsy-turvy fella.

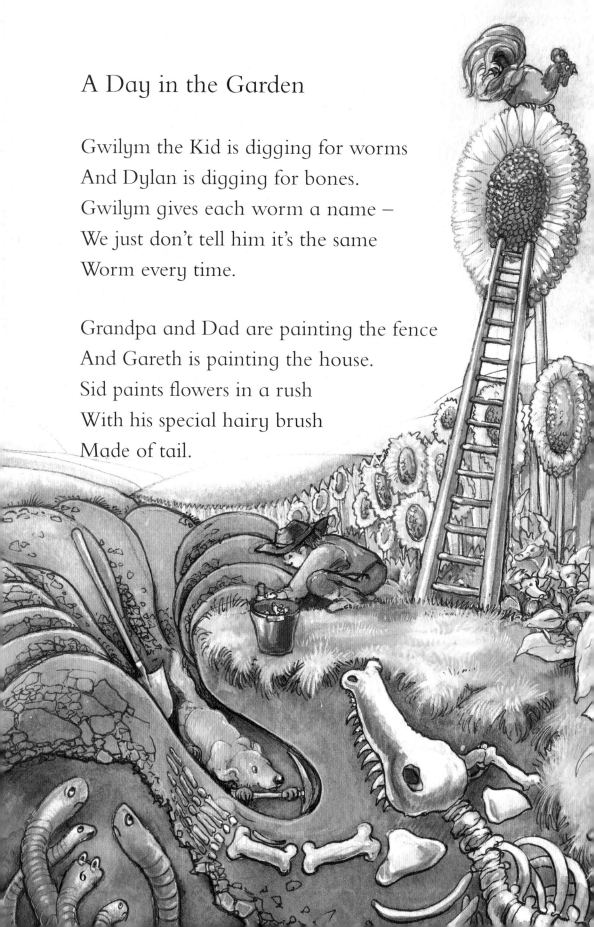

A Day in the Garden

Gwilym the Kid is digging for worms
And Dylan is digging for bones.
Gwilym gives each worm a name –
We just don't tell him it's the same
Worm every time.

Grandpa and Dad are painting the fence
And Gareth is painting the house.
Sid paints flowers in a rush
With his special hairy brush
Made of tail.

6

Mam and Beth are practising serves
And Nana is serving the tea.
Pickled pancakes, chocolate plums
Sausage biscuits, popcorn buns . . .
Gone, but for crumbs.

Gareth and Mam have cleared away
And Nana has cleared off with Gramps.
Bethan and Dad are taking a thorn
From Dylan's paw, so out on the lawn
The only ones left
Are . . .

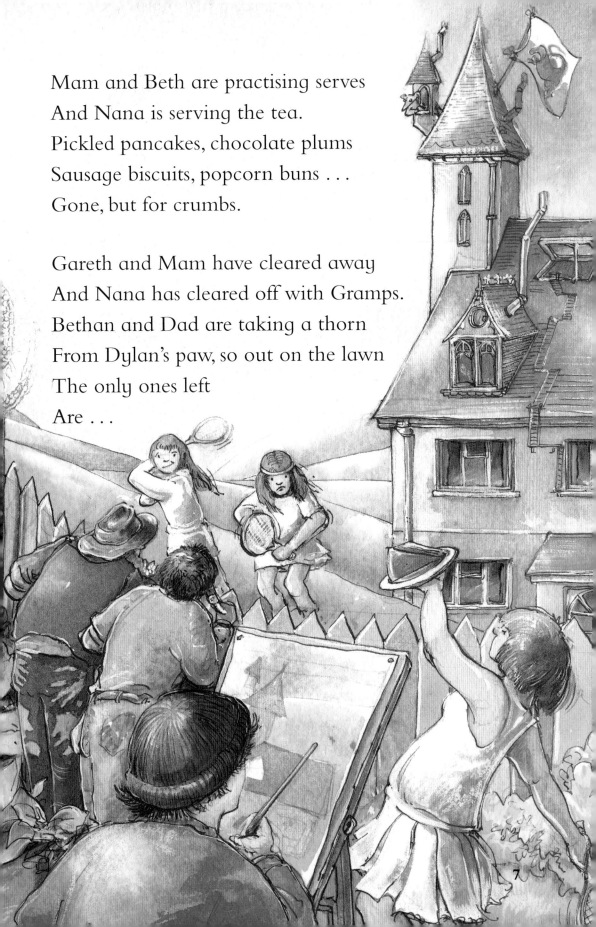

Seeking Silver

I climbed Da's ladder and I stretched up high
To take the silver from the sky
But each star was too far and all I could reach
Was a lone goose feather fluttering by.

I rowed Da's boat on stream and spring
To skim the silver surface gleam
But all I trawled from the rippling rings
Was a tiny fish with silver wings.

My Gramps bent down his shiny head
For me to pluck a silver thread
(His present from the crescent sky)
My search is over . . . thank you, moon.

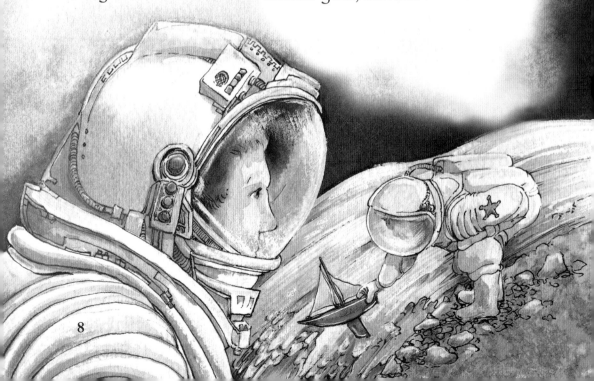

Sid's Day Out

Step outside, Sid,
Into a green surprise
Dappled in sunlight.

Step outside, Sid,
To blues of cloudless skies,
Everywhere leaves and flowers.
Paws – don't pause – hurry now!

Outside home you can roam
Under an endless sky.
Time to move past the door –
Sid, you were destined for
Ice-cream clouds, chocolate trees,
Dancing leaves, daring deeds.

Everything waits for you –
Step outside, Sid.

Gwilym and Grandpa

My Grandpa says it, so it must be true,
　There was a time in olden days
　When he was little, too.

He wore short trousers when he went to school;
　I wonder if he had his beard
　When he was little, too.

He has a wallet with keys inside
　And umpty pairs of spectacles;
　He's very wide.

Was Grandpa really once like me?
Was he really small?
How did his eyebrows get so thick?
How did he grow so tall?

If my Grandpa says it, then it must be true . . .
I'm going to be a Grandpa, too.

Faces to Places

The train from Neath is driven by Keith
Who stops at Merthyr for Auntie Bertha
And picks up Dave at Abercrave,
And then he gets Benny from Abergavenny.

Clare pays her fare at Aberdare
And stands by Mandy at Tonypandy.
Milly and Billy get on at Caerphilly
And ask: 'Is it far then
To go to Carmarthen?'

From station to station
On wheels and on rails:
Our destination? . . . The whole of Wales!

Twins

Like fish in a glass bowl or ships out at sea
We pass, never touching, my brother and me.
Like birds in the air, like trains on the line
Our paths never mingle, my sister's and mine.

He likes peanut butter and strawberry jelly
Both in the same egg roll . . . talk about smelly!
She loves runny yoghurt; I say it's like vomit.
I'm crazy for blue cheese; she'd run a mile from it!

I say 'Get it done now'; he says 'Take your time'.
I relish surprises; he likes words that rhyme.
We twins are quite different – we're rarely the same.
I think life's a drama; she thinks it's a game.

But when Gwilym bleeds from a cut on his knee
Or Sid's in big trouble, stuck high up a tree
Or Dylan is lonely and wants company . . .
We act as one person . . . my brother and me.

The Witches go Shopping

Good morning to you, Bela Gwrach
What would you like today?
I'd like ten grams of laughing spells, a packet of assorted smells
A drink to make me disappear, a chocolate cake that lasts all ye
And twenty purple mynah birds with morning's song to sing.

Good morning to you, Menna Gwrach
What will you have today?
I'd like a giant jar of sleep, twelve baby dragons going 'cheep'
A bar of jam, a jar of soap, a skipping chair, a rocking rope
And twenty purple mynah birds with morning's song to sing
And thirty golden honeybees without a single sting.

Good morning to you, Eira Gwrach
What will you buy today?
I'd like a can of fizzy screams, a bottle of forgotten dreams
A slice of never-ending bread (so all the mynahs can be fed)
And twenty purple mynah birds with morning's song to sing
And thirty golden honeybees without a single sting
And forty silver butterflies with eyes upon each wing.

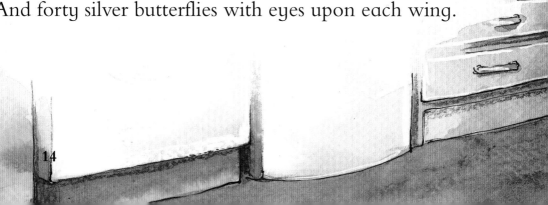

Teifion's Leek

Searching here and searching there
We are searching everywhere.
Someone's taken Teifion's leek
That his Auntie grew last week.

Searching here and searching there,
Teifion says, 'It's just not fair!'
We are playing hide and seek.
Who has hidden Teifion's leek?

Leeks are green, but Cai is red.
'Very sorry, Miss,' Cai said.
'You'll not find that leek … you see
Teifion's leek is inside me!'

Reading Lessons

There's a star in the custard
And a rat in the grate
There's a boa in the cupboard
And a bat in debate.

There's an ache in my teacher
And an ear in my heart
All this reading is so tricky
That I don't know where to start.

17

Dancetime

Sing me a song for I wish to dance,
I shall spin dust, I shall stir rain,
I shall fashion a whirlpool out of air
And twirl to your music again and again.

Darkness

Darkness does not frighten me
Nor night nor shadows
Nor the velvet whispering of bats
In the deepening air
For I am the cat with the silent paws
And I do not easily scare.
  BEWARE . . .
You creatures who creep while humans sleep
You creatures who fly in a starless sky
In the black night air
For I am the cat with the silent paws
And I do not easily scare.

Canal Walk

Along the water's margin where slow horses used to pull
Dogs take their owners for a stroll
A jogger runs past on a roll
A whizzing cyclist rings his bell
And there is no-one left to tell the tales of long ago.

Atop the mottled water where canal boats used to plough
Black water boatmen flail their oars
Slow ripples ring the watercourse
Carpets of lilies float downstream
And there is no-one left to dream the tales of long ago.

Beside the silver water where coal barges used to wind
We sit and let the day float by
Beneath a green and leafy sky
And wonder how and what and why
Of olden times and days gone by when *now* was long ago.

The Jelly Sea

I tread the peanut-butter sand
Until I reach the jelly sea
Where ice-cream trickles through the waves
– I wish I'd brought my spoon with me!

I climb the fudgy trudgy cliffs
Where chocolate shadows come and go
And watch where fizzy water laps
Butterscotch pebbles far below

And as I splash the jelly sea
And race along the sherbet dunes
And climb the chocolate-covered fudge
– I wish I'd remembered those spoons!

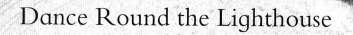

Dance Round the Lighthouse

Roll up the sand, roll up the sea,
Mumbles beach is the place to be,
Bring down the moon, bring down a star,
Time for a party, whoever you are.

Bring down a star, bring down the moon,
Everyone's going to be dancing soon.

Roll up the sea, roll up the sand,
Dance round the lighthouse, hand in hand.

Fly in the clouds, swim in the sky,
Wash all the stars and hang them to dry.

Sing all night to a seashell tune,
Dance round the lighthouse, dance round the moon.

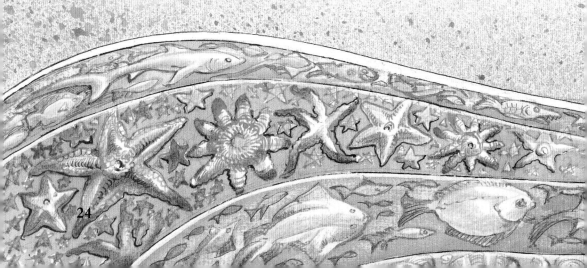

25

Growing Things

I bought seven packets of crocodile seeds,
They were blue and purple and they looked like beads.
I sowed them deep when the stars were low
And I sang them scales to help them grow.

First came the flowers, purple and blue
With petals like tongues and nectar like glue
And from each centre, without fail,
Each flower sported a crocodile tail.

The stems were orange and the leaves were white
And when I touched them they curled up tight.
And when my friends came round, I said,
'To look at those tails costs 2p a head.'

One dark night, when a blue moon shone,
I crept into the garden and called for Mum
For there in the moonlight, orange, gold and green,
Were the tiniest crocodiles you've ever seen.

Now they feed on the reeds in the goldfish pool
Those tiny shiny crocodiles are just so cool.
Cat, dog and hamsters: those pets are fine
But I'm buying octopus seeds next time.

What Would They Do?

What would they do without Dylan?
What would they do without me?
Who'd bark at the postman?
Or pee on his van?
Who'd sniff every lamppost –
Not Gareth nor Nan!

What would they do without Dylan?
What would they do without me?
Who'd guard little Gwilym?
Or sleep in Dad's chair?
Who'd eat all the dog-food
If I wasn't there?

What would they do without Dylan?
What would they do without me?
Who'd take Dad for walkies?
And pester the cat?
Who'd lick Mam and Bethan?
And chew Grandpa's hat?

Oh, they couldn't do without Dylan!
No, they couldn't do without me!

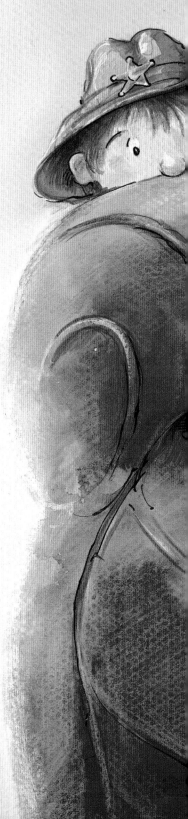

The Sleepmaster

When darkness cloaks valleys in grey
And shadows climb over the wall,
When night puts an end to the day
The Master of Dreams comes to call.

And as you drift off towards sleep
He comes to the foot of your bed
'May I interest you in a dream
Or maybe a nightmare instead?'

If you opt for a magical dream
You'll think it a pity to wake.
Asleep, you will fly in a rose-tinted sky
Or sail on a whale in a lake.

But if you take nightmares to bed
You'll run from a poisonous snake,
You'll quiver with fear as monsters draw near
But oh, the relief when you wake!

When darkness leaves valley and hill
And dawn's sun draws light from the moon,
The Master takes flight with his trappings of night
But whispers, 'Be seeing you soon.'

First Impression – 2004

ISBN 1 84323 328 2

© text: Nicola Davies
© illustrations: Elaine Franks

Nicola Davies and Elaine Franks have asserted their rights under
the Copyright, Designs and Patents Act, 1988, to be identified
as Author and Illustrator of this Work.

This title is published with the financial support
of the Welsh Books Council.

Cover design: Olwen Fowler

Printed in Wales at Gomer Press, Llandysul,
Ceredigion, Wales SA44 4JL